*Quick*GUIDES

everything you need to know...fast

Sources of Funding

by Jill Ritchie

reviewed by Caroline Hukins

WIREMILL
PUBLISHING LTD

Across the world the organizations and institutions that fundraise to finance their work are referred to in many different ways. They are charities, non-profits or not-for-profit organizations, non-governmental organisations (NGOs), voluntary organisations, academic institutions, agencies, etc. For ease of reading, we have used the term Nonprofit Organisation, Organisation or NPO as an umbrella term throughout the *Quick*Guide series. We have also used the spellings and punctuation used by the author.

Published by
Wiremill Publishing Ltd.
Edenbridge, Kent TN8 5PS, UK
info@wiremillpublishing.com
www.wiremillpublishing.com
www.quickguidesonline.com

Copyright ©2004 Wiremill Publishing Ltd.

All rights reserved. No part of this publication may be reproduced or utilised in any form or by any means, electronic or mechanical, including photocopying, recording or by any information storage or retrieval system without the prior written permission of the publisher.

British Library Cataloguing in Publication Data
A catalogue record for this book is available from the British Library.

ISBN Number 1-905053-05-3

Printed by Rhythm Consolidated Berhad, Malaysia
Cover Design by Jennie de Lima and Edward Way
Design by Colin Woodman Design

Disclaimer of Liability
The author, reviewer and publisher shall have neither liability nor responsibility to any person or entity with respect to any loss or damage caused or alleged to be caused directly or indirectly by the information contained in this book. While the book is as accurate as possible, there may be errors, omissions or inaccuracies.

CONTENTS

INTRODUCTION

Charities, nongovernmental organisations, academic institutions and other nonprofit organisations (collectively referred to in this Guide as NPOs) across the world raise funds in different ways from a wide range of sources with new opportunities continually emerging.

This Guide identifies the diverse sources that provide funding to NPOs. It will inspire new ideas and help your organisation diversify its income base. If an organisation is dependent on a few sources of income, it puts itself at risk of serious damage should one of them underperform. By investing in a range of fundraising methods and targeting different audiences, this risk is substantially reduced.

What sources of funds would be suitable for your organisation? What sources might your organisation be missing? Consider the following range of donors to NPOs. How many are you deriving money from or even investigating? Be imaginative. The following sections cover many possible sources of funding, but there may be more. Share information with colleagues and other NPOs to find out about other possibilities.

Evaluating the Sources of Funding

Most NPOs raise funds from some or all of the following sources:

- Individuals
- Communities, including community groups
- Companies
- Groups and associations
- Trusts and foundations, i.e., grantmaking bodies
- Government and quasi-government sources
- Sales activities, including sales of goods, services and fees
- Investments

The choice as to which sources are most appropriate for an organisation will depend on many factors including: the nature of the cause, the size of the organisation, the remit of the charitable work, the existing supporter base, the nature of current fundraising, and the volunteer or staff skills available.

Planning which funding initiatives to introduce and when to introduce them should form the basis of your fundraising strategy, depending on the factors that are unique to your organisation.

The largest share of income for many NPOs comes from contributions by individuals.

FINDING DONORS

Individual donors may be recruited by letter, email, telephone, TV appeal, radio appeal, leaflets left at homes or offices, or advertisements. Anyone is a potential donor. However, targeting those who are more likely to give will increase the return on investment. Consider, for example, people who have the means to give, who may be giving to similar organisations, and/or who may have some affiliation with your cause (e.g., a relative of someone who recently died at a hospice as a potential donor to the hospice).

Those organisations fortunate enough to have alumni or graduates or a natural constituency such as visitors to a museum or theatre don't have to seek potential donors because the potential donors come to them. They can focus attention on ensuring maximum participation and funding from these contacts.

Reviewer's Comment
Members of the governing body (board members, trustees, governors, etc.) should be considered as possible donors. However, you need to be sensitive to local customs. In some countries, there is definite pressure on board members to make a financial commitment to organisations they help govern; in others it's just the opposite, and board members may expect to be paid for their time. In any event, because members of the board will be those involved most closely with your organisation, it is worth considering them as a group of potential donors or as a group that can suggest donors to your organisation.

TYPES OF DONATIONS

Donors can give donations by cheque, credit card, bank transfer and, of course, cash. They can also give property. Shares of stock are often popular, as are donations of clothing or household items for resale. Anything is possible if the donor wants to give it and the NPO is willing to receive it. Regular donations are ideal because they guarantee future income, minimise administration, and help an NPO to plan its work with some confidence of future income levels. However, single donations are also valuable, and these donors can often be converted to making regular contributions. Often there will be a tax-effective way for donors to give and NPO staff should make themselves aware of these laws. Tax benefits associated with donations to NPOs can encourage larger gifts or more numerous ones.

Reviewer's Comment
A donation of property may be particularly subject to tax benefits and specific rules. Though property can be a useful source of funds when it is sold, ensure that you understand all of the issues surrounding the gift including legal, insurance, and restrictions on use or sale before accepting the donation.

MEMBERSHIPS
Signing people up as members of your organisation serves both to generate money and to upgrade the members' involvement with the organisation from that of a mere donor to a person with a formal connection to the organisation. Memberships imply something extra, special and even elite. Members' benefits do not need to cost your organisation a lot of money – they may simply be privileges such as attendance at certain events or voting rights or they may be more extensive depending on what works best for your organisation

You may choose to devise a plan with tiers of donors giving at different levels, and receiving a package of communications or benefits tailored to the level at which they give.

MAJOR GIFTS
Major gifts are large donations to the organisation. Major gifts may come from members of the organisation's governing body or other committed and wealthy supporters. Many NPOs separate donors who have given above a certain level or have the

Continues on next page

potential to do so in order to communicate with them more personally. This means the relationship with such people becomes closer, and they often become deeply involved in the NPO's work.

It can take months or years of work to identify and cultivate donors of major gifts, but this can ultimately be rewarded by a significant donation. In addition to major financial support, these donors can help by introducing other valuable contacts to the NPO.

DONATIONS AT DEATH
(Legacies and Bequests)

Individuals can support the organisation by leaving it funds or property in their wills. These legacies and bequests generally take effect at the donor's death. Many organisations actively market bequest and legacy giving to their donors. An advantage of donations at death is that they can often be larger than gifts made during life particularly if the donor has no family or the family is otherwise financially provided for.

Reviewer's Comment

Bequests and legacies are the same thing – they are just known under different names in different countries. There may be substantial tax benefits associated with donations at death. You need to ensure that you know what these are and communicate them to potential donors.

Clearly the subject must be approached sensitively as many people do not like to talk about or think about death, but many people are more than willing to provide for a cause that is important to them when planning their will. But it is vital to nurture existing donors to encourage them to make a bequest.

EVENTS

Individuals who are not willing to give a donation to an NPO may be willing to pay to attend an event put on by that organisation. Some supporters will happily do both. They may be encouraged to attend a ball, dinner, garden party, sporting event, auction, race night, exhibition, or preview ... there are no limits and the event need not have any connection with the work undertaken by the organisation.

Maximise the opportunity that attending an event affords. Apart from the ticket price to enter, you can raise additional funds through sales of products or raffle tickets, and through auctions, games or collections during the event. The captive audience could be shown a brief presentation about your organisation in order to interest them in your work. Names and contact details can be gathered from ticket sales or the collection of business cards for future communication. Materials about the organisation, including a request for funds, can be given to each person attending an event.

SPONSORED ACTIVITIES

Individuals may take on a challenge or activity through which they can raise sponsorship for your cause. Examples are races, cycle rides, walks, bungee jumps, having a beard shaved off or abstaining from doing something for a period of time. Generally the participant asks friends, family, colleagues or others to give a certain amount of money for completion of the task. These may be activities that your NPO organises such as sponsored races, or you may promote independently organised events such as running a marathon. Some people may choose to organise their own activity or event as well as seeking sponsorship for participating in it.

COMPETITIONS/RAFFLES

Competitions or raffles are events whereby someone buys a ticket in order to try to win a prize. They can be run on an organised nationwide basis, or as local activities. Nationwide, they require a large number of volunteers, each selling a significant number of tickets, and they rely on attractive prizes to be successful. Local ones will generally be much less ambitious in scope. Games, competitions and raffles are often governed by strict regulations, so find out about local laws before committing time and resources. Most well-run NPO raffles, lotteries or other contests have a dual

Continues on next page

role of making money and gathering the contact details of entrants. Most people who enter competitions are gamblers rather than potential donors to your cause, but having their contact details allows you to educate them about your cause and convince them to become donors or otherwise become involved in its work.

VOLUNTEERS AND STAFF

Handled sensitively, people who already give their time and effort to the cause may also make financial contributions. You don't want to seem ungrateful for their volunteer activities, but they need to be made aware that the organisation needs financial as well as their other support.

If asked, they may consider making a donation, attending an event, leaving a bequest, or other financial involvement with the organisation.

Paid staff may also want to support the organisation for which they work through donations or other financial involvement.

Reviewer's Comment

It is important to remember that all these sources of potential individual support are not mutually exclusive.

Members might upgrade their membership to a higher level, or they might respond to a major gift appeal.

Regular donors may attend an event or take part in a sponsored activity.

People committed enough to consider a major gift may equally consider leaving a legacy.

The vast majority of people who give to NPOs do so simply because they are asked. So don't be afraid to keep asking. Offer well-timed, exciting opportunities which serve to deepen an individual's involvement with the organisation because the more someone is involved with an organisation, the more likely he or she is to support it financially.

There are dozens of opportunities to raise money in your local community by drawing on local support: pub quizzes; collections in the street, supermarket, local shops or restaurants; used-clothing or household-goods sales; school fundraising initiatives; garden parties; and visits to local attractions are among the many possibilities. Most work best when a committed group of volunteers active in the local community is willing to organise and staff the event.

Reviewer's Comment
Pub quizzes are events whereby participants in a local bar or pub form teams that are asked a number of questions (sometimes with a theme sometimes not) and the team that knows the most answers wins. They can be hugely profitable fundraising events and highly fought between teams. They are a great example of a local event as most of the participants will be local and know each other. It provides a lot of publicity for the NPO as well as fun for the participants.

PROJECTS
Money can also be saved for your organisation by asking local people to undertake project work for which you would otherwise have to pay (for example, painting a new centre, clearing a littered or environmentally damaged area, driving a minibus for the elderly or disabled). This type of work often fosters a real sense of belonging among your volunteers, and between your volunteers and your organisation. Again, it is the local element that often makes it possible to ask for and receive this type of support.

SCHOOLS
Schools can help in a number of ways. For example, all the 14-year-olds' classes can organise an annual fair and donate the proceeds to your organisation; the school as a whole can have a special dress day where everyone wears something different than usual (e.g., fancy dress costumes or blue shirts or purple hats); or volunteers might take on a fundraising project such as a sponsored walk where the children obtain sponsorship for walking a specific distance, a sponsored silence where sponsorship is obtained for the

Continues on next page

period of being quiet or a spell-a-thon where sponsorship is obtained for each word spelt correctly.

COLLECTIONS

A significant amount of money can be raised by sustained collection-tin initiatives where collecting boxes or plastic receptacles are left for coins or change in shops, taken door-to-door or to work, or "rattled" by volunteers in public places.

Tins can be placed in stores, railway stations, airports, office reception areas, and theatres – anywhere people congregate and particularly where they handle money, subject to local laws and regulations.

Reliable and trustworthy voluntary help is the key to a successful collection-tin project because the volunteers will generally be those who distribute and collect the boxes or receptacles in local areas. Not only do you need to be able to trust the volunteers with funds but they also must be willing to collect the boxes on a regular basis. Volunteers willing to stand and "rattle" a box for funds will need to have the time to do so and the willingness to be ignored by large numbers of people.

Reviewer's Comment
Public activities including collections may be subject to a range of laws and regulations. There may be requirements placed on the organisation including insurance needs, identification of volunteers, permits and so forth.

Ensure you find out what is required and follow all rules and regulations.

GROUPS AND ASSOCIATIONS

SOCIAL CLUBS

Many clubs that people join for social purposes also undertake fundraising projects for good causes. These may be the local bridge club, the Girl Scouts, a sports group, the Rotary or other civic group, or any of the many other clubs that bring people together. The club itself may adopt an NPO and make a donation from its own funds or organise events in aid of the NPO, or it may allow the NPO to solicit donations from its members. Clubs can be approached at a national or local level depending on the NPO or project to be supported.

Club members frequently take on practical projects (for example, creating a play park for children and paying for and helping to erect the equipment, putting up or repairing fences, planting grass and trees, or establishing flower gardens). Generally people like to see a tangible result from their efforts somewhere close to home. Club members also tend to like projects with plenty of time to raise the required funds.

FAITH-BASED GROUPS

Churches and other religious congregations can be approached for either direct financial support or for their constituents to undertake a project. Faith-based groups or congregations usually have large numbers of volunteers who can offer hands-on help, either for the direct benefit of those whom your organisation serves or for an event (e.g., marshals for a road race or manpower for a street collection).

It is worth establishing whether the specific church, school, mosque, synagogue or other religious organisation would insist on beneficiaries being of the same faith. The religious views of the NPO's board and staff might also be an issue. However, more and more faith-based groups today are supporting good causes without first regard to religion.

COMPANIES

There are a variety of ways in which a company can support your organisation. By approaching a company correctly, you may be able to access any or all of the following sources of funds within the same company.

MARKETING BUDGET

Supporting an NPO can bring a company tangible benefit in terms of positive PR, increased sales, or access to its target audience. This may be achieved by the company sponsoring a publication or activity, or through cause-related marketing (for example, packaging can state that an amount or percentage per bottle of drink sold will benefit the NPO – benefiting the drink's manufacturer with increased sales and the NPO with income). Marketing funds are spent based on the return for the company; it is not a purely philanthropic decision. The NPO needs to make a sound business case for such support.

ADVERTISING BUDGET

A company may pay the NPO to advertise in the NPO's publications or pay the NPO to send promotional material about the company or its products to the NPO's database of beneficiaries or supporters.

SPONSORSHIPS

Companies are invited to give a fixed amount of money in exchange for a range of benefits. These benefits may include:

- Promotion of company name and association with the sponsored project
- Access to NPO's brand and supporter base
- Logo and name acknowledgments
- Company employee benefits
- Corporate entertaining

DONATIONS

The company simply makes a donation and receives nothing in return. There may be tax benefits either to the company or the NPO, depending on local laws.

A company may donate by matching fundraising by its staff. This may be matching donations with a donation from the company. Or the company may match donations of time by employees with cash donations from the company. Or if an employee, for example, runs a marathon, the company may match the amount raised by the employee. All of these matching opportunities encourage community involvement by staff and staff support by the company.

GIFTS-IN-KIND

Rather than giving cash, a company might make another gift that benefits the charitable organisation. Donations-in-kind could be anything – foodstuffs, cleaning materials, stationery, premises, furniture, equipment, or prizes for competitions or events. Often in-kind donations are of products produced by the company for sale.

Alternatively, companies may offer expertise at a discounted rate. Accountants, lawyers, management consultants, trainers, electricians, IT specialists or any other professional could be asked to provide services for a reduced rate or for free.

EMPLOYEES

Employees may be encouraged to take part in payroll giving. This entails a representative of the NPO addressing staff members directly about the work of the organisation and offering them the opportunity to donate. Those who sign up for the plan agree that donations will be deducted from their salaries by their employers. There may be tax benefits to the donor or the NPO, depending on local laws.

Employees may be invited or given some incentive to attend fundraising events. Employees may also be encouraged in their charitable activities by matching-gift programmes whereby the company matches, with funds, the donations or volunteer hours given by employees.

Some companies may encourage staff to do voluntary work for your NPO. Alternatively, they may offer a staff member to work for your organisation for a period of time, thus saving staff costs.

There is a growing trend worldwide for companies to "lend" senior employees to NPOs. Thus, a corporate marketing manager or a head of public relations could be asked to develop a marketing strategy for your organisation, or a staffing problem could be handled by a corporate human-relations person with conflict-resolution skills – all at no charge to the NPO.

Continues on next page

CUSTOMERS

Companies can give invaluable help to your NPO by granting you access to their customers. For example, companies can include a leaflet in a mailing to customers, promote the sale of NPO products in stores, include advertisements in publications sent to customers, invite customers to a fundraising event or encourage them to take part in a sponsored activity.

CORPORATE-FUNDED TRUSTS AND FOUNDATIONS

For legal and tax reasons, some companies form foundations or trusts through which charitable donations are made. They are usually, but not always, named after the company. Such companies retain close links with these foundations or trusts and usually give a certain amount to the foundations or trusts annually for disbursement to NPOs. There is likely to be an application procedure to be followed in order to access these funds.

"NPO OF THE YEAR" ADOPTIONS/PARTNERSHIPS

Many large companies manage their charitable giving by selecting one NPO each year that will benefit from an organised programme of fundraising and support. This can include any or all of the previously mentioned fundraising methods and usually entails considerable PR benefits as well. The company may expect to benefit significantly from the association in terms of positive PR and recognition, or it may simply use fundraising events to increase staff motivation and facilitate team building. There is strong competition for such partnerships.

Reviewer's Comment

To find out a company's policy on charitable support, look first on its Website or approach it and ask for information. To make a successful bid for support, you will need a thorough understanding of the company's relevant objectives and its decision-making processes, plus a long lead time to interest the company in your cause and build the relationship. In order to maintain and extend a partnership, it is important to ensure the relationship is meeting the company's objectives.

COMPANIES

Once a company has a relationship with you, even if it is only by making one type of donation, be sure to ask if it would be interested in helping in other ways. A company that gives an annual donation may well take out advertising in a magazine, offer event places to employees, or permit payroll giving to be pitched to its staff.

ALL COMPANIES WORTH APPROACHING

It is also worth investigating small businesses, medium-sized companies and public utilities. Public companies are state-owned or quasi-state companies, often providing utilities such as water, electricity, transport, or telephone service. They may give donations, sponsorships or gifts-in-kind to NPOs.

Many medium-sized companies are also approachable for financial support. The founder of such a company is often working actively in the business, and social investment decisions may be based on his or her personal preferences such as school, university, personal interests, or geographic location. Often a personal

experience can determine such an entrepreneur's giving criteria for his or her company – a relative lost to cancer may result in funding for cancer research or care, for instance.

Do not neglect smaller local businesses, either. Even someone running an enterprise from home is a potential supporter and may give money, voluntary time or a donation of the product or service that he or she offers. Local businesses are often much more supportive of local causes than big companies.

Trusts and foundations (legal entities established for the purpose of making grants) exist in many countries to support NPOs. Trusts and foundations range from large internationally known entities with substantial resources to small local organisations. They have the advantage of being known and frequently available to receive applications for funding.

Many trusts and foundations have rigid grant-making criteria dictated by their constitutions or specific interests determined by their governing body. Some are restricted to supporting specific types of organisations. For instance, some grant-making may only support domestic NPOs or NPOs that look after animals, children's organisations or environmental causes. On the other hand, many trusts and foundations have broad grant-making interests and leave specific grant-making decisions to the discretion of their staff. In many cases, trusts and foundations only support causes in a specified geographic area.

Research is vital to ensure that you approach trusts or foundations likely to be interested in the work you want funded and that you approach them with an appropriate application at the right time. The process of research, application preparation and a decision by the grant-making can be a long one.

Reviewer's Comment
Trustees or board members of grant-making may, as individuals, also make personal donations or introduce other potential supporters to your cause. Look for the wider opportunities that might be available as part of your contact with grant-making bodies. Also look for a long-term relationship. If a foundation or trust has given
once, be sure to ask again, unless of course this goes against its giving criteria.

GOVERNMENT AND STATUTORY SOURCES

Governments may fund an NPO when the NPO's service or product is acknowledged to be a government responsibility but the NPO is better placed to deliver it. A sum is awarded usually yearly with numbers of conditions attached.

SUBSIDIES
One system of government support is to give the NPO a fixed amount per person or animal helped by the NPO.

GRANTS
Grants are usually applied for by NPOs for a specific programme to be funded in its entirety by the governmental body. Obtaining such grants often entails a lot of research and paperwork.

PARTNERSHIPS
Government partnerships with NPOs generally mean the governmental body will provide some of the service and the NPO other parts of the service. In this manner, the goals of both the NPO and government are fulfilled and less expensively than if either party had to provide the entire service.

WORK PLANS
Local or national governments may run initiatives that provide people for an NPO free of charge in order to give them work experience while helping a good cause.

Reviewer's Comment
This type of government initiative may be very specific to only a few countries. Other countries may have different initiatives that will also benefit NPOs. See what is available for you.

LOCAL GOVERNMENT
Local governments may be able to give an annual grant or subsidy to a local project, or provide access to related trusts or foundations that are able to do so.

Reviewer's Comment
Remember that any relationship with local or national government gives your NPO access to influential individuals who may become donors personally or be able to introduce you to other influential people with a personal interest in your cause.

COMMERCIAL ACTIVITIES AND FEES FOR SERVICES

BENEFICIARIES/CLIENTS
It is often acceptable, even expected, to charge beneficiaries a fee.
A museum may charge for entry, or a literacy organisation might charge for books.

MEMBERS
Members may pay for some member benefits including subscriptions and goods purchased through a gift shop or online catalogue. The member still pays but is given a reduced price.

CUSTOMERS
Many NPOs provide products or services to beneficiaries for free or at discounted rates, but also offer their services or products at full price to the corporate sector and to individuals who can afford to pay. An example would be training courses or counselling in interpersonal skills.

PREMISES
Can you profit from renting your premises when not in use (for example, university accommodation during student holidays or a conference-room facility)? This can provide an excellent source of funds for the NPO, often with little associated cost.

TENDERS
By law many governmental bodies are required to put work out to tender, thereby giving all suppliers or contractors a fair chance of quoting on a job or service. NPOs that have the infrastructure, experience and ability can apply for such tenders as a means of generating income. Anything can be put out to tender, from running a tearoom in a municipal park to the removal of alien vegetation from nature reserves.

MERCHANDISE
An NPO may sell merchandise with its name on it (mugs, T-shirts, etc.) and/or sell unrelated goods, either directly or through commercial companies offering such programmes.

NPO SHOPS
Many organisations collect donated clothing or other items and sell this merchandise through retail shops.
In some cases premises may even be donated.

INVESTMENT INCOME

If your organisation has money held in reserve that is not to be spent immediately, more money can be made from investing it wisely.

Advice should be taken from financial advisors and other professionals.

Items to consider when contemplating investments are the rate of return, security of investments, saving plans, and returns on noncash assets such as property.

Earning money on investments can be very beneficial to your organisation but may also contain pitfalls because most investments can reduce in value as well as increase.

APPEALS

An appeal is a fundraising event that combines many of the previously mentioned fundraising methods, generally held over a limited period of time with the aim of funding a specific vision or project. Successful appeals have a clear case for support; a defined time frame and target; and the commitment of key staff, trustees and volunteers. An appeal would involve fundraising events, corporate support, and applications to trusts and foundations,

An appeal is usually chaired by a voluntary committee of well-connected and committed individuals, willing to make personal donations and to use their influence and contacts to promote the cause.

Reviewer's Comment
Appeals with media backing are a huge advantage. The key to getting media backing is usually a personal relationship with influential individuals. Always be on the lookout for who knows whom among your supporters. Failing personal relationships, an attractive proposition properly presented may attract media interest, particularly for timely causes.

Conclusion

Regardless of your NPO's size, there is a range of fundraising opportunities to support your activities.

An effective fundraising strategy will consider all of these sources of funding and will select a mix that is pragmatic and effective for the NPO concerned. When choosing which funding sources to pursue, consider the cost and ease of implementation, the likely returns, and the workload likely to be generated.

A strong fundraising department will pursue a range of funding sources, so that the impact is less severe if one or two initiatives should fail. However, trying too many sources and spreading investment too thinly can simply mean that none of your fundraising methods are given a good chance of success. These decisions need to be made by staff and the board and reviewed regularly to ensure opportunities are not missed. Circumstances change, both within the organisation and in the wider world.

Even small NPOs should ensure they know all the possible sources of funds and take advantage of them as appropriate. Sometimes one activity will come to the fore, and sometimes another will.

Any organisation worthy of being supported should ensure that all potential supporters have the opportunity to support it as broadly and deeply as possible.

JILL RITCHIE

Jill Ritchie started her own business at the age of 18 while also studying. By the time she was 28, she had created jobs for 120 people in a factory with seven retail outlets. At the same time, she was spending more time doing voluntary charity work than anything else. She then closed her business and entered the NPO sector as a member of the start-up team of the Triple Trust, the highly successful South African job-creation organisation, where she initially trained trainers and ran the organisation's marketing arm. After a year there, she took over the fundraising and, in five years, took the Triple Trust from a budget of South African Rand 100,000 per annum to Rand 9 million, most of which was raised from northern hemisphere donors. Jill left to start her own fundraising consultancy and book-publishing business, which she has run for the past 15 years. She has edited 3 books and written 15, 12 on fundraising, of which the best known is *Fundraising for the New Millennium.*

She has arranged numerous successful events for South African NPOs, raising both funds and friends for the organisations in the process. She has achieved much success in the field of cause-related marketing.

Jill is Vice President of the Southern Africa Institute of Fundraising and also heads up its Ethics Committee. She is in demand around the world as a speaker on fundraising.

Caroline Hukins, Reviewer

Caroline Hukins has worked in the non-profit sector in the UK for more than 10 years, both as a volunteer fundraiser and a professional.

Following university, she won a place on the National Society for the Prevention of Cruelty to Children (NSPCC) graduate trainee program in Fundraising Appeals, and subsequently worked on the multimillion-pound Full Stop Campaign for the Millennium. She spent 18 months organizing overseas biking and trekking challenges for Macmillan Cancer Relief, generating over $1 million from this type of fundraising. She then spent 3 years managing a wide-ranging events program at the National Asthma Campaign, which includied sporting events, overseas challenges, sponsored activities, ticketed special events and wider community fundraising.

Caroline now works as a freelance author and editor, and leads charity treks and bike rides all over the world.